POLICY FRAMEWORK FOR BILATERAL FOREIGN AID

U.S. Agency for International Development

Contents

Foreword

The publication of this policy paper formally signals the change in strategic direction that I sought for the United States Agency for International Development when I became Administrator five years ago. It affirms that we will seek to use bilateral foreign assistance to build toward a safer and more secure, democratic, and prosperous world to enhance our own national security. Implementing this policy will make U.S. bilateral aid more effective and better coordinated with other U.S. Government policies and programs.

> We will seek to use bilateral foreign assistance to build toward a safer and more secure, democratic, and prosperous world to enhance our own national security.

The National Security Strategy of the United States, published in September 2002, asserted that development is as critical to national security as defense and diplomacy. The challenge for bilateral foreign assistance—and for USAID as the principal U.S. Government foreign assistance agency—was to turn that assertion into a reality. With the publication of this policy paper, USAID signals its transformation into a renewed international development agency responding to an altered global development landscape.

At the same time that the National Security Strategy was revised, USAID published *Foreign Aid in the National Interest*. The motivation for and message in this analytical document was that there was an altered context for U.S. foreign assistance. It summarized the challenges and opportunities we saw as we stood on the threshold of the 21st century.

We saw that there would be important global and national dimensions to expanding democratic governance, promoting economic growth and poverty reduction, improving people's health, mitigating conflict, providing humanitarian aid, and taking better account of private foreign aid flows. Some parts of this landscape were familiar, and we had the tools to go to work right away. Other ground was newer, and required some real changes in the way foreign assistance had been used in the years since George C. Marshall conceived a new role for foreign aid immediately following World War II.

We spent the next two years consulting widely and thinking deeply about the changes in this context and how we might best move in new directions for bilateral foreign assistance. This led to the publication of *U.S. Foreign Aid: Meeting the Challenges of the Twenty-first Century,* the Agency's first White Paper, in January 2004. This paper was USAID's own effort to shape the discourse and decisions on the way forward in the 21st century. It emphasized the importance that countries play in their own development and reminded us that foreign aid supports country progress, rather than leading it. So, our aid will have the most development impact when used in countries that do the most to help themselves.

The White Paper acknowledged, however, that U.S. foreign aid has other core goals besides transformational development, each with its own guiding principles. However, the paper asserted that the United States must speak with one voice to be heard in the new global environment. To the extent foreign aid carried the message, our aid needed to have a few, clear, concise goals consistent with larger U.S. foreign policy objectives, yet these goals must express the full range of what we do. Thus was born the concept of articulating five core goals and aligning resources and results with those goals.

Among those goals was something relatively new for bilateral foreign assistance: a recognition that weak or fragile states required special attention and a different strategy for assistance than our familiar objectives and tools for transformational development or humanitarian response.

January 2005 saw the publication of USAID's *Fragile States Strategy,* which calls for a thorough understanding of the sources of fragility in a country. To tackle those sources of fragility, USAID's country assistance strategies will enhance stability, improve security, encourage reform, and develop the capacities of essential institutions in vulnerable and crisis countries. We are already seeing the effects of the *Fragile States Strategy* in the design of our country programs and the first progress reports from the field.

Our strategic realignment to respond to the U.S. National Security Strategy positions USAID to implement the highest foreign policy objectives of President Bush, including the Global War on Terror and the Freedom Agenda. Assisting frontline states of the war on terror in reconstruction and development has been the focus of a major effort over the past four years, and we have had some significant successes. The Freedom Agenda is predicated on the shared understanding that democracy promotion is central to our national identity and directly in the national interest of the United States. Thus, USAID promotes democracy and good governance in support of all five of the core goals, and USAID's core goals likewise fully support the Freedom Agenda. *At Freedom's Frontiers: A Democracy and Governance Strategic Framework,* published in December 2005, elaborates USAID's role in implementing the Freedom Agenda.

The *Policy Framework for Bilateral Foreign Aid* brings together our work over the past five years in a single document and inscribes in policy USAID's change in strategic direction. It positions USAID in broader discussions of the role of foreign aid—not only in the United States, but around the world with our many partners in development. It also serves as an agenda for the work that will be needed to make the policy fully operational. The policy will guide USAID as we take up the development mandate for the betterment of others and our own national security.

Andrew S. Natsios

Andrew S Natsios
USAID Administator
January, 2006

Executive Summary

The 2002 National Security Strategy identified development as one of the three cornerstones of U.S. national security, along with defense and diplomacy. Further, as a result of globalization, increased interdependence, the end of the Cold War, and other trends and events, the term "development" now covers a much wider array of interests and concerns than it did during the 1970s and 1980s. The expanding agenda for

> This policy provides the overarching framework for the Agency's strategies and policies and for USAID strategic planning, budgeting, and programming.

foreign aid has posed serious challenges to policy coherence. The increasingly complex and multifaceted nature of development and foreign aid have also posed a challenge for the United States and other donors in making aid as effective as possible.

This policy focuses on the strategic management of U. S. bilateral foreign aid. To improve policy coherence and address both real and perceived issues of

effectiveness, this policy identifies, clarifies, and distinguishes among USAID's core strategic goals; calls for a clearer alignment of resources with each goal; and establishes principles for strategic management to achieve results in terms of each goal. It thereby provides the overarching framework for the Agency's strategies and policies and for USAID strategic planning, budgeting, and programming.

USAID's policy framework is based on five core strategic goals for foreign aid:

1. *Promote transformational development:* Promote far-reaching, fundamental changes in governance and institutions, human capacity, and economic structure, so that countries can sustain further economic and social progress without depending on foreign aid. This goal pertains to reasonably stable developing countries, with emphasis on those with significant need for concessional assistance and with adequate (or better) commitment to ruling justly, promoting economic freedom, and investing in people.

2. *Strengthen fragile states:* Reduce fragility and establish the foundation for

development progress by supporting stabilization, security, reform, and capacity development in countries characterized by instability and weak governance, when and where U.S. assistance can make a significant difference.

3. *Support strategic states:* Help achieve major U.S. foreign policy goals in specific countries of especially high priority as key allies from a strategic standpoint.

4. *Provide humanitarian relief:* Help meet immediate human needs, save lives, and alleviate suffering in countries afflicted by violent conflict, crisis, natural disasters, or persistent dire poverty.

5. *Address global issues and other special, self-standing concerns:* Undertake activities that relate to concerns such as HIV/AIDS and other infectious diseases, climate change, biodiversity, direct support for international trade agreements, and counter narcotics efforts. Almost all of these concerns affect development. But these kinds of activities are typically undertaken for their own sake (hence "self-standing"). They call for distinct approaches to resource allocation and results reporting.

To implement this framework, USAID will identify and distinguish among the resources and programs that address each of these goals. USAID will align budgetary resources according to which of the five goals these resources primarily support, and will manage these resources accordingly.

For each goal, resources will be allocated among countries based on criteria that promote aid effectiveness and results in terms of that goal. The criteria for determining allocations to countries will vary, depending on the goal. Similarly, within countries, resources will be allocated to the activities that promise to yield the best results in terms of the goal under which these resources fit. Again, the guiding principles for resource allocation within countries may vary from goal to goal, depending on what principles are most important for effectiveness and results in terms of each goal.

For each goal, graduation criteria will be established that

- indicate what assistance is supposed to accomplish

- help define need

- serve as a guide to programming

- provide a basis for judgments about when the job has been accomplished and aid for the particular goal or concern can cease

Implementation of this policy would be greatly facilitated by a new set of accounts for foreign aid that correspond to the five core goals. In the absence of new accounts, however, the policy can be implemented by internal measures to align the resources in existing accounts with the core goals and manage those resources accordingly.

Policy Framework for Bilateral Foreign Aid

Introduction

This policy focuses on the strategic management of U.S. bilateral foreign aid. Foreign assistance addresses a large number of goals and objectives. It is important to measure results and success against the relevant objective. To improve policy coherence and address both real and perceived issues of effectiveness, this policy identifies, clarifies, and distinguishes among USAID's core strategic goals; calls for a clearer alignment of

> In recent years, development and foreign aid have become more important, as well as more complex and multifaceted.

resources with each goal; and establishes principles for strategic management to achieve results in terms of each goal. It thereby provides the overarching framework for Agency strategies and policies, and for USAID strategic planning, budgeting, and programming.

Background

In recent years, development and foreign aid have become more important, as well as more complex and multifaceted. The 2002 National Security Strategy identified development as one of the three cornerstones of U.S. national security, along with defense and diplomacy. There has been a concomitant expansion in U.S. bilateral foreign aid, including two major initiatives—the Millennium Challenge Account and the President's Emergency Plan for AIDS Relief.

Further, as a result of globalization, increased interdependence, the end of the Cold War, and other trends and events, the term "development" now covers a much wider array of interests and concerns than it did during the 1970s and 1980s. The agenda for foreign aid has expanded accordingly to include global and transnational issues; the transition from communism; crisis, conflict, and complex emergencies; and many other more specific concerns.

The expanding agenda for foreign aid has posed serious challenges to policy coherence. Studies of U.S. foreign aid since the late 1980s all emphasize problems of policy incoherence—multiple and often conflicting goals and objectives—along with excessive direction and restriction that hamper USAID's capacity to make the best use of its resources to achieve development results. While there is considerable variation in the proposed solutions, there is a remarkable degree of unanimity on the diagnosis.[1]

The increasingly complex and multifaceted nature of development and foreign aid have also posed a challenge for the United States and other donors in making aid as effective as possible. Many of the guiding principles that make sense for the more traditional part of the development and foreign aid agenda are less applicable when addressing some

of the other important concerns that have emerged over the past 15 years—strengthening fragile states, supporting key allies in the war on terrorism, mitigating HIV/AIDS, addressing climate change and other global issues, dealing with complex emergencies, and others.

Aid effectiveness in each distinct area calls for correspondingly distinct approaches to program planning, resource allocation, implementation, and evaluation. It also requires new models of aid delivery, such as public-private alliances, which extend the Agency's reach and effectiveness in meeting objectives by combining USAID's strengths, resources, and capabilities with those of other institutions, including businesses, foundations, civil society and other governments.

This policy establishes a new framework for bilateral foreign aid that responds to these important changes and challenges. It identifies and distinguishes among the core goals that foreign aid should address in support of the U.S. National Security Strategy and U.S. national interests. For each goal, the policy identifies distinct guiding principles for program planning, resource allocation, implementation, and evaluation to increase aid effectiveness and achieve better, clearer results.

This policy is based on the analysis and conclusions of USAID's White Paper *U.S. Foreign Aid: Meeting the Challenges of the Twenty-first Century* and on the discussion, debate, and analysis carried out since it was presented in draft at the October 2003 USAID Mission

Directors' Conference.[2] The Agency and the Department of State are collaborating to reflect the goals established in this paper in revisions of the 2004–2009 State-USAID joint Strategic Plan.[3]

Core Goals for Bilateral Foreign Aid

USAID's policy framework is based on five core goals for foreign aid:

1. *Promote transformational development:* Promote far-reaching, fundamental changes in governance and institutions, human capacity, and economic structure so that countries can sustain economic and social progress without depending on foreign aid. Such development is the most effective approach for reducing poverty, promoting gender equality, ensuring environmental sustainability, and achieving other Millennium Development Goals on a lasting basis. This goal pertains to reasonably stable developing countries, with emphasis on those with significant need for concessional assistance

---

1 See Lee Hamilton and Benjamin Gilman, *Report of the Task Force on Foreign Assistance to the Committee on Foreign Affairs, U.S. House of Representatives* (Hamilton-Gilman Report), February 1989, (Washington, D.C.); George M. Ferris et. al., *The President's Commission on the Management of AID Programs: Report to the President—An Action Plan* (Ferris Report), April 1992 (Washington, D.C.) <http://pdf.dec.org/pdf_docs/PCAAA222.pdf>; Clifton R. Wharton Jr. et. al., *Preventive Diplomacy: Revitalizing AID and Foreign Assistance for the Post-Cold War Era—Report of the Task Force to Reform AID and the International Affairs Budget* (Wharton Report) September 1993 (Washington, D.C.); and more recent analyses: Development Assistance Committee, *Development Co-operation Review: United States* (Paris: Organization for Economic Cooperation and Development, 2002); Jim Kolbe, "Lessons and New Directions for Foreign Assistance," *The Washington Quarterly*, 26, 2 (Spring 2003); and Steven C. Radelet, *Challenging Foreign Aid: A Policymaker's Guide to the Millennium Challenge Account* (Washington, D.C.: Center for Global Development, 2003).

2 USAID, *U.S. Foreign Aid: Meeting the Challenges of the Twenty-first Century*, White Paper (Washington, D.C.: USAID, 2004) <www.usaid.gov/policy/pdabz3221.pdf>. The White Paper, in turn, built on *Foreign Aid in the National Interest: Promoting Freedom, Security, and Opportunity* (Washington, D.C.: USAID, 2002) <www.usaid.gov/fani/>; *The National Security Strategy of the United States of America*, 2002 <www.whitehouse.gov/nsc/nss.pdf>; the Monterrey Consensus <www.un.org/esa/ffd/aconf198-11.pdf>; work associated with the Millennium Challenge Account; and other seminal contributions.

3 U.S. Department of State and USAID, *Strategic Plan Fiscal Years 2004–2009: Aligning Diplomacy and Development Assistance*, 2003 <www.usaid.gov/policy/budget/state_usaid_strat_plan.pdf>.

and with adequate (or better) commitment to ruling justly, promoting economic freedom, and investing in people.

2. *Strengthen fragile states:* Reduce fragility and establish the foundation for development progress by supporting stabilization, security, reform, and capacity development in countries characterized by instability and weak governance, when and where U.S. assistance can make a significant difference.

3. *Support strategic states:* Help achieve major U.S. foreign policy goals in specific countries of especially high priority as key allies from a strategic standpoint.

4. *Provide humanitarian relief:* Help meet immediate human needs, save lives, and alleviate suffering in countries afflicted by violent conflict, crisis, natural disasters, or persistent dire poverty.

5. *Address global issues and other special, self-standing concerns:* Undertake activities that relate to concerns such as HIV/AIDS and other infectious diseases, climate change, biodiversity, direct support for international trade agreements, and counter narcotics efforts. Almost all of these concerns affect development. But these kinds of activities are typically undertaken for their own sake (hence "self-standing"). They call for distinct approaches to resource allocation and results reporting. They are often distinguished by directives that are

restrictive rather than broad, and call for detailed program guidance about the uses of funds. Some centrally driven initiatives also belong under this goal insofar as they are treated by USAID as independent, self-standing concerns for purposes of strategic management.

To implement this policy framework, USAID will identify and distinguish among the resources and programs that address each of the five core goals. This calls for differentiating country programs according to which of the first three goals the program primarily addresses.[4] It also calls for identifying resources that address global issues and other special concerns.[5] More generally, USAID will align budgetary resources with the goal they primarily support, and will manage them accordingly. This process will necessarily be iterative, reflecting information and guidance that accumulate over the course of the budget cycle as well as changes in country circumstances.

The policy can be implemented by internal measures to align resources in existing accounts with the core goals, and then manage those resources in accordance with guiding principles for each goal. Although a new set of accounts for foreign aid that correspond to the five core goals would be advantageous, policy implementation is possible under

the present account structure.[6] For each goal, resources will be allocated among countries based on criteria that promote aid effectiveness and results. For instance, the allocation of transformational development resources will take overall country commitment and need heavily into account, since these have an important bearing on aid effectiveness and development results. The criteria for determining allocations to countries will vary, depending on the goal.[7]

Similarly, within countries, resources will be allocated to the activities that promise to yield the best results in terms of the goal under which these resources fit. Again, the guiding principles for resource allocation within countries may vary from goal to goal, depending on what principles are most important for aid effectiveness and results. For instance, recipient ownership and partnership are important guiding principles for transformational development activities. These factors may not play the same role in assistance to fragile states with recalcitrant governments or for humanitarian assistance.

---

4   See PPC/P, "Methodology/Approach—Country Groups," Draft, April 2005.

5   See PPC/P, "Criteria for Identifying Special Concerns, Including Global Issues," Draft, March 2005.

6   See, for example, USAID, FY 2006 Congressional Budget Justification <www.usaid.gov/policy/budget/cbj2006/summaryofbudgetrequest_06.pdf>. See also PPC/RA, "Supplement to the Guidance on FY 2007 Bureau Program and Budget Submissions," May 2005.

7   In some cases, the criteria may be similar but the weights attached may be different. For instance, foreign policy criteria are primary for programs in support of key allies and development policy performance is, at best, a secondary consideration. This ordering would be reversed for transformational development country programs. For global issues and other special concerns, need and commitment often come into play, but these are defined in terms of the specific concern rather than in broad development terms.

For each goal, graduation criteria will be established. These will indicate what assistance is supposed to accomplish, help define need, serve as a guide to programming, and provide a basis for judgments about when the job has been accomplished and aid for that particular goal or concern can cease.

- *For transformational development states,* these criteria typically have to do with economic and social indicators, such as per capita income, life expectancy, literacy, and fertility—indicators that essentially gauge the level of development and figure in many calculations of country need.

- *For fragile states,* the appropriate criteria and indicators relate to political instability, vulnerability to conflict and crisis, and basic governance—indicators used to gauge the degree of fragility.

- *For strategic states,* graduation criteria are specific to each country and the strategic concern that motivates the aid program.

The remainder of this paper discusses each goal; the types of resources that correspond to the goal; and general principles for strategic budgeting and programming, results reporting, and graduation. This provides the general framework within which more detailed guidance will be formulated and provided.

Goal 1: Promote Transformational Development[8]

Goal

The goal is to support lasting development progress, with a predominant focus on countries that are reasonably stable, need foreign aid, and are committed to development progress—as evidenced by policy performance in the areas of ruling justly, promoting economic free-

> The ultimate goal is for countries to reach a level of development such that they can sustain further progress on their own, without relying on foreign aid.

dom, and making sound investments in people. The ultimate goal is for countries to reach a level of development such that they can sustain further progress on their own, without relying on foreign aid. Countries would then graduate from developmental foreign aid.

---

8   The terms "development" and "transformational development" are used interchangeably in this section of the paper, though with full recognition that the five core goals all support "development," as discussed in *The National Security Strategy* and elsewhere.

Resources

Resources for transformational development are those which are flexible enough to be allocated across countries as well as within countries, based on broad development criteria. Such resources would be subject to—at most—very broad sectoral earmarks or directives and very flexible program guidance. Resources subject to relatively restrictive earmarks, directives, and programmatic guidance will be managed as part of global issues and other special self-standing concerns.

Resources from the Millennium Challenge Account (MCA) promote transformational development in a limited number of countries and in response to specific country proposals. There remains a clear need for other resources to promote transformational development in other countries, including a significant number with good policy performance that are not MCA-eligible. Further, to the extent that MCA programs are tightly focused and limited in scope, there is a strong argument for complementary USAID transformational development programs in MCA-recipient countries. It is to these USAID resources that the following principles apply.

Strategic Budgeting

USAID will identify annually those countries where country programs primarily address transformational development (as opposed to countries where the primary focus is fragility or support for key strategic allies). USAID will distinguish among countries in this group according to income level—low-income and middle-income—and policy performance, using readily available, sound measures used by the Millennium Challenge Corporation (MCC), the World Bank, and others.

A share of transformational development resources will not be allocated to countries, but will be used for central bureaus and "global public goods" (such as agricultural research) that primarily serve development goals.

Of the development resources available to be allocated to countries, USAID will identify the share that should go to middle-income countries for transformational development programs (as opposed to resources in middle-income countries for global issues and other special concerns covered under the fifth goal).

Allocations of resources for low-income countries will take commitment and policy performance heavily into account, along with need (as reflected in development indicators) and population size. Program performance, foreign policy importance, and other relevant criteria will also influence allocations. To the extent transformational development resources are relatively scarce, USAID will focus these resources mainly on low-income countries that are good performers. Transformational develop-ment programs in countries that are only fair or weak performers will be relatively modest. They will be focused on a more limited set of activities that build a foundation for improvements in governance—both to help strengthen performance and to avoid instability and fragility.

MCA-eligible countries may enter into compacts with the MCC that result in significant development programs. As these countries enter into compacts, USAID will review needs, opportuni-ties, and implications for USAID-funded development programs. USAID will also consider programs for other core goals—particularly global issues and other special concerns—in MCA-eligible countries. In good performers that have been designated MCA "thres-hold countries," USAID will program resources as in other good performers, while also paying attention to specific areas that would help prepare these countries for potential MCA eligibility.

Regional bureaus may make intra-regional adjustments to country alloca-tions based on more specific judgments about policy performance, program performance, and other development considerations, in consultation with the Bureau for Policy and Program Coor-dination (PPC). Regional bureaus may also request transformational develop-ment resources for regional programs or projects that are primarily justified by development criteria and primarily focused on development results. These might address transnational issues of critical importance from a transforma-tional development standpoint, such as regional infrastructure or water.

As emphasized, this process will neces-sarily be iterative, reflecting information and guidance that accumulate over the course of the budget cycle as well as changes in country circumstances.

Country Strategies and Programs

Missions will formulate medium-term country assistance strategies for pro-gramming these funds, based on the following principles and practices:[9]

- support recipient efforts to rule justly, promote economic freedom, and invest in people

- maximize development results and impact, based on country needs, op-portunities, and priorities

- emphasize country ownership and participation in formulating and designing aid programs

- take full advantage of partnerships with other donors, governments, communities, nongovernmental organizations, the private sector, and universities

- give priority attention to policies, institutions, and absorptive capacity

- take into account activities of other donors

- work within a common, country-owned framework

---

9 "Medium-term" is roughly a three- to five-year time span, as discussed in the *Interim Strategic Management Guidance,* December 2004 <www.usaid.gov/policy/ads/200/updates/iu2-0412.pdf>. For more detail on guiding principles for effective assistance, see the annex.

- focus on achieving graduation criteria and thresholds

Strategies will have a limited number of strategic objectives, with program components under each that link directly with the USAID-State Joint Strategic Plan.

Results

Missions will report on expected and actual results. Programs should be assessed in terms of progress in ruling justly, promoting economic freedom, and investing in people, as well as progress toward the development outcomes embodied in graduation criteria.

Graduation

USAID will formulate criteria and indicators to guide judgments about whether and when a transformational development country no longer requires development resources. Such criteria might permit graduation by sector, up to the point where all criteria are met.

Graduation from development resources does not mean that all aid would stop. A development graduate might receive assistance for global issues and other special concerns; for humanitarian purposes; for foreign policy reasons; or to address fragility.[10]

For countries considered close to graduation, USAID will formulate general guidance regarding criteria for assistance activities, the transition to graduation, and mechanisms for a post-graduation relationship, such as endowments and foundations.[11]

---

10 The evidence and empirical record suggest that fragility mainly affects low-income countries. Indeed, the models used to assess vulnerability to conflict and instability get much of their predictive power by using indicators that distinguish poor countries from others, and the Agency's progress thus far in grouping countries according to primary program goals tends to confirm this. Nonetheless, there are significant elements of fragility in some middle-income countries that may need to be addressed.

---

11 These issues will be analyzed and addressed in a forthcoming USAID middle-income country strategy.

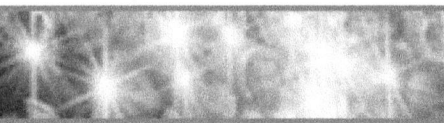

	PROMOTE TRANSFORMATIONAL DEVELOPMENT	**STRENGTHEN FRAGILE STATES**
GOAL	*USAID will support progress in ruling justly, promoting economic freedom, and making sound investments in people until countries can sustain further development on their own, independent of foreign aid.*	*USAID will support stability, security, reform, and capacity development in fragile states as the foundation for long-term development.*
ELIGIBILITY	Reasonably stable, needy countries committed to lasting development progress	Countries lacking sufficient foundation for long-term development due to instability and weak governance
STRATEGIES AND PROGRAMS	• emphasize country ownership and participation • work in a common, country-owned framework to prioritize policies, institutions, and absorptive capacity • take advantage of partnerships and complement work of other donors	• enhance stability and improve security • advance reforms related to conditions driving fragility • develop basic infrastructure and capacity of essential institutions
STRATEGIC RESOURCE MANAGEMENT	Resources are allocated across and within countries based on need, policy performance, program performance, and other development considerations, with the first two criteria being most important. Some resources are made available for regional and central activities.	Resources are flexible and, at most, subject to very broad sectoral direction. Allocations are based on criteria that include vulnerability to conflict and crisis, commitment of host governments or significant nongovernmental actors, foreign policy importance, and program performance. Some resources go to central and regional programs.
RESULTS	Programs are assessed in terms of progress in ruling justly, economic freedom, and investing in people.	Programs are assessed in terms of how well they enhance stability, improve security, advance reforms, and develop capacity.
GRADUATION	When a country no longer needs development resources, though assistance toward other goals in the framework could continue	When country circumstances move above a threshold set using fragility criteria and indicators; graduates typically move to transformational development programs

	SUPPORT STRATEGIC STATES	PROVIDE HUMANITARIAN RELIEF	ADDRESS GLOBAL ISSUES AND OTHER SPECIAL, SELF-STANDING CONCERNS
GOAL	*USAID will support and help to advance the U.S. foreign policy objectives that motivate the assistance.*	*Regardless of the character of the government in a given country, USAID will help save lives and alleviate suffering.*	*These are concerns and issues that USAID pursues for their own sake, rather than as part of larger transformational development considerations. They often call for concerted response that is focused on a subset of countries where the issue or concern is acute.*
ELIGIBILITY	Countries where U.S. foreign policy concerns call for significantly higher aid levels and/or different program content than justified by development or fragility criteria	Countries afflicted by violent conflict, crises, natural disasters, or persistent dire poverty	Goals, objectives, and priorities that USAID pursues as largely independent, self-standing concerns (such as HIV/AIDS prevention and treatment and global climate change)
STRATEGIES AND PROGRAMS	• vary from country to country, depending on broad program goals and underlying foreign policy concerns • in consultation with the Department of State, program goals selected that best serve the motivating U.S. foreign policy objective	• reinforce USAID interests in other goal areas and promote follow-on development efforts • are guided by the concept of relief that promotes recovery and livelihoods and the principle of doing no harm • as appropriate, address both immediate and protracted need for humanitarian assistance, and develop mitigation and prevention programs	• are tailored to each concern, including performance monitoring approaches, outcome indicators, and accomplishments • may be identified and addressed at global, regional, or country levels • may have global or regional plans with little or no opportunity to respond to host country plans in implementation
STRATEGIC RESOURCE MANAGEMENT	Funding, usually from ESF and similar resources, is based primarily on foreign policy criteria. Resources are usually free of earmarks and directives. Strategic states may also receive funding for global issues and humanitarian relief.	Resources—including PL 480 Title II Emergency Food Aid and International Disaster and Famine Assistance—are allocated to countries with immediate, urgent need for humanitarian assistance, taking into account the capacity of the recipient to meet its own needs. Resources may also go to promoting local and regional capacity to respond to emergencies.	Resources are typically specified in earmarks, directives, and initiatives. USAID also directs funding to special concerns, largely based on concern-specific criteria. Program performance also influences allocations.
RESULTS	Assessments of overall success consider the program's contribution to the foreign policy objectives that motivate it.	Assessments are based on the objectives of saving lives, directly alleviating hunger and suffering, reducing the economic impact of disasters, and laying the groundwork for follow-on development efforts.	Expected and actual results are reported, using appropriate indicators for the concern or issue.
GRADUATION	When foreign policy concerns no longer warrant exceptional program levels and/or influence program content	When humanitarian assistance is no longer needed	When the specific criteria formulated for each concern are met

Goal 2: Strengthen Fragile States[12]

Goal

Fragile states are countries where instability and weak governance do not provide sufficient foundation for long-term development. Most are low-income countries. Some are considered to be in crisis, while others may be characterized as vulnerable.

> USAID will periodically identify countries where country programs should primarily focus on fragility, based on the level of instability, vulnerability to conflict and crisis, and the quality of governance.

The goal is to support stability, security, capacity development, and reform, thereby helping fragile states to become transformational development countries and good performers. This would constitute graduation.

Resources

Resources for fragile states are those which are flexible enough to be allocated across countries as well as within countries, based on fragile states criteria. To permit flexibility, such resources would be subject to (at most) very broad sectoral direction.

Strategic Budgeting

USAID will periodically identify countries where country programs should primarily focus on fragility (rather than development), based on the level of instability, vulnerability to conflict and crisis, and the quality of governance. For these countries, USAID will analyze the nature and sources of fragility and the potential for external assistance to make an impact.

USAID will allocate resources to selected fragile states based on vulnerability to instability, conflict, and crisis; commitment by the host government and/or significant nongovernmental actors; the feasibility of achieving results; and foreign policy importance. Actual program performance will also influence allocations.

Some fragile states resources will go to central or regional programs, rather than to countries. These funds could be used to support transnational initiatives

---

12 See USAID, *Fragile States Strategy* (Washington, D.C.: USAID, 2005) <www.usaid.gov/policy/2005_fragile_states_strategy.pdf>.

aimed at reducing fragility and improving regional stability, and to support individual country activities from regional or central platforms. The funds could also be used for central support activities, such as operational research and early warning and monitoring systems.

Country Strategies and Programs

Given the instability and volatility of most fragile states, missions will formulate near-term strategies within the framework established by USAID's *Fragile States Strategy*.[13] This strategy calls for the identification of situations likely to lead to conflict, crisis, and state failure, with particular focus on weak governance as a driver of fragility. Mission strategies will be based on analysis and demonstrated understanding of sources of fragility and the ability of USAID programs to affect these conditions, taking into account the activities of other donors.

USAID's programmatic goals in fragile states will be to enhance stability in political, economic, and social arenas; improve security, including personal security; advance reforms that address the conditions that drive fragility; and develop capacity of essential institutions and basic infrastructure. Programmatic priorities will depend upon the degree of fragility and the direction

in which the country is headed. The key is to ensure that programs focus on the sources of fragility, demonstrate near-term impact, and lay the foundation for long-term recovery. When a fragile state is vulnerable, the focus will likely be on capacity building and reform, in response to governance issues. When a fragile state is in crisis, the strategic focus will be on stabilizing the situation, enhancing security, and mitigating the potential for conflict or the impact of conflict.

Strategies will have a limited number of strategic objectives, with program components under each that link directly with the USAID-State Joint Strategic Plan.

Results

Missions will report on expected and actual results. Programs should be assessed based on results, in terms of enhancing stability, improving security, advancing reforms, and developing capacity, as well as progress toward the outcomes embodied in graduation criteria.

Graduation

Decisions about graduation will be based on fragility criteria, indicators used to identify fragile states, and informed judgments. Graduates would typically move to a primary focus on transformational development programs, based on the guiding principles discussed in the previous section.

---

13 See also USAID, *ADS 201—Planning* <www.usaid.gov/policy/ads/200/201.pdf>.

Goal 3: Support Strategic States

Goal

Strategic states are those where U.S. foreign policy concerns and interests call for significantly higher aid levels than would be justified by development or fragile states criteria and/or where program content may be heavily influenced by these same foreign policy concerns. The goal is to support and help advance the foreign policy objectives that motivate the assistance. This may call for programs aimed at development progress, programs that address fragility, or other kinds of programs.

> Strategic states and programs are distinguished by the heavy influence of foreign policy concerns on overall program levels and program content.

Strategic states and programs are distinguished from those discussed previously by the heavy influence of foreign policy concerns on overall program levels, program content, and USAID's capacity to adhere to guiding principles discussed in the previous two sections. Graduation would similarly be determined by reference to the foreign policy concerns that motivated the assistance in the first place.

Resources

Funding for strategic states is typically from Economic Support Fund (ESF) and similar resources. To support foreign policy concerns, these resources are usually flexible and free of the earmarks and directives associated with special development concerns. Strategic states may also receive funding for global issues and other special concerns, as well as for humanitarian relief.

Strategic Budgeting

Identification of countries and funding levels are typically determined mainly by the Department of State, the National Security Council, and/or Congress, with significant USAID input. Funding levels are generally determined primarily by foreign policy criteria and—at best—secondarily by need, commitment, performance, or other development or fragility criteria.

Country Strategies and Programs

For each country program, broad goals and objectives need to be worked out in close consultation and cooperation with the Department of State. Considerations include

- the program goals that best serve the U.S. foreign policy interests underlying the overall program, including promoting transformational development or reducing fragility

- the feasibility of achieving development results or diminished fragility in a particular country context and the kinds of programs likely to be most effective[14]

Country strategies will vary from country to country, depending on broad program goals and objectives and underlying foreign policy concerns. In some cases, strategies might closely approximate transformational development or fragile states strategies. In other cases (such as Israel, Turkey, and Ireland) a strategy may not be warranted, though an operational plan might be called for.

Strategies will have a limited number of strategic objectives, with program components under each objective that link directly with the USAID-State Joint Strategic Plan.

Results

Missions will report on expected and actual results, using appropriate indicators that reflect programmatic goals and objectives. However, there will be clear recognition of contextual factors—including constraints posed by foreign policy concerns and recipient commitment—that might influence and limit results. Overall success will be assessed, first and foremost, in terms of the contribution of USAID's program to the foreign policy objectives that motivate the aid program.

Graduation

Criteria for graduation will be specific to the country in question, and will depend on the foreign policy concern that motivates the assistance (and not on development indicators or fragility indicators per se). A country will graduate when foreign policy concerns no longer warrant exceptional program levels and no longer have a significant influence on program content.[15]

Country strategies or other program documentation will discuss the criteria for judgments about graduation, so that the rationale for the program is clear and aid effectiveness is judged by relevant criteria.

---

14 Much has been made of potential and actual conflicts between development concerns and foreign policy concerns that often motivate ESF—the classic case is Zaire under Mobutu. However, there has been growing recognition since the 1980s that the strength of the U.S. partnership with many key strategic allies often depends on the recipient government's willingness and capacity to achieve genuine development progress for its people. A recent PPC/P review covering major aid recipients since 1965 indicates that a significant number of countries with foreign policy-driven aid programs have made substantial development progress.

15 For instance, increased stability in the Balkans has led to a sort of graduation, as a number of country programs have become significantly less foreign policy-driven over the past five years.

Goal 4: Provide Humanitarian Relief

Goal

Humanitarian response is a longstanding foreign aid priority. The goal is to help save lives and alleviate suffering of people in distress, regardless of the character of their governments. This includes programs aimed at preventing disaster and famine. Humanitarian programs depend on need. They may be pursued in countries where the main program focus is transformational development;

> Resources are allocated to countries based on immediate, urgent need for humanitarian assistance.

in those where fragility is the main concern; in those where country programs are primarily motivated by foreign policy concerns; or in other countries that do not normally receive foreign assistance.[16]

Resources

Humanitarian aid currently includes PL 480 Title II Emergency Food Aid and International Disaster and Famine Assistance.[17]

Strategic Budgeting

Resources are allocated to countries based on immediate, urgent need for humanitarian assistance, taking into account the capacity of the recipient to meet its own needs. Resources for prevention are also allocated mainly on the basis of need.

Strategies and Programs

The need for country planning for humanitarian aid is determined on a case-by-case basis. In many instances, only an operational plan is called for. Strategic planning will be required for countries where the need for humanitarian assistance is not only immediate and urgent but persistent, so that humanitarian assistance is expected to be provided

---

16 This is well illustrated by the humanitarian aid associated with the December 2004 tsunami.

17 In countries afflicted by persistent dire poverty and food insecurity, it remains unclear under which goal to place assistance that meets immediate human needs in non-emergency situations.

on a protracted basis. Strategic planning is also required for mitigation and prevention programs that reduce risks associated with disasters.

Humanitarian assistance is often provided to countries where USAID is concerned with other goals, such as transformational development, overcoming fragility, and combating HIV/AIDS and other communicable diseases. Humanitarian assistance will be provided in ways that reinforce the Agency's interests in these other goal areas and set the stage for follow-on development efforts.

Similarly, USAID is guided by the "do no harm" principle that seeks to ensure that humanitarian assistance does not have unintended negative consequences, such as instability, dependency, or increased beneficiary risk. The concept of relief that promotes recovery will be integrated into the programming of humanitarian assistance. Humanitarian programming will promote livelihoods, as well as social, civic, and economic recovery.

USAID will promote local and regional capacity to respond to emergencies, thereby mitigating the impact of disasters and reducing the need for external assistance.

Through the Department of State and the United Nations, the Agency will encourage diplomatic resolution of issues of displacement or impending displacement, providing durable solutions for those affected.[18]

Strategic objectives for humanitarian response link directly with the USAID-State Plan, which includes humanitarian response as a strategic goal.

Results

Humanitarian programs will be assessed based on the objectives of saving lives, directly alleviating hunger and suffering, reducing the direct economic impacts of disasters, and laying the groundwork for follow-on development efforts.

Graduation

Graduation will take place when there is no longer a need for humanitarian assistance.

---

18 See USAID, *Assistance to Internally Displaced Persons Policy* (Washington, D.C.: USAID, 2004) <http://pdf.dec.org/pdf_docs/PDACA558.pdf>

Goal 5: Address Global Issues and Other Special, Self-Standing Concerns

Goal

This goal area encompasses the many other goals, objectives, and priorities that USAID pursues as largely independent, self-standing concerns. Almost all of these concerns contribute to development. Nonetheless, they are typically pursued largely for their own sake, and are not subordinated to larger transformational development considerations and criteria.

> These concerns are typically pursued largely for their own sake, and are not subordinated to larger transformational development considerations and criteria.

Examples of global issues include HIV/AIDS, certain other infectious diseases, and climate change. Some regional issues may also be included under this goal, such as programs directly aimed at countering narcotics or other illicit trade and direct support for U.S. trade agreements. Other special, self-standing concerns may be country-specific, rather than global or regional. Such concerns often call for a concerted response that focuses on a subset of countries where the issue or problem is most acute or immediate.

Need and (often) commitment in terms of the specific concern are the major criteria for funding, rather than general development need and overall commitment to good governance. These concerns can be pursued in transformational development countries, fragile states, and strategic states. They are pursued in programs for which the broad principles discussed under transformational development or fragile states are not readily applied.[19]

Resources

The resources for this goal area are typically specified in earmarks, directives, and initiatives emanating both from Congress and the administration. USAID also directs funding to special

---

19 See PPC/P, "Criteria for Identifying Special Concerns, Including Global Issues," Draft, March 2005. A major ongoing task has been identifying the activities and funding that belong in this goal area, as opposed to the four others, particularly transformational development.

concerns over the course of budget and program process.[20]

Strategic Budgeting

For each issue or concern, the corresponding resources will be allocated according to criteria specific to the concern or issue. These criteria may include need and commitment, but in terms specific to the concern in question. For instance, HIV/AIDS resources are allocated based on criteria—such as problem severity and magnitude—that pertain directly to HIV/AIDS.[21] Program performance will also play a role in determining allocations.

Strategies and Programs

Strategic planning and performance monitoring approaches will be tailored to each concern to reflect outcome indicators and accomplishments at country, regional, or global levels, as appropriate. For some special concerns and global issues, it may be appropriate to develop global or regional plans and performance monitoring, especially when the concerns are Washington-driven and individual operating units have little or no opportunity to respond to country plans during implementation.

Strategic objectives that include global issues and other special self-standing concerns can usually readily be associated with goals and objectives in the USAID-State Joint Strategic Plan.

Results

Operating units will report on expected and actual results, based on appropriate indicators specific to each issue or concern. Since many special concerns stem from particular administration or congressional interests, expectations for reporting may be more intense than for other programs, with attendant implications for program and staffing resource requirements. USAID will make every effort to avoid duplicate reporting requirements for a given activity or concern.

Graduation

Criteria for graduation are specific to the concern in question. Criteria will be formulated for each concern to make the purpose of the assistance more transparent and ensure that aid effectiveness and graduation are judged by appropriate indicators.

---

20 Not all earmarks, directives, and initiatives would count as special concerns; it depends on how narrowly focused and restricted the resources are. Similarly, some programs that address global public goods (such as agricultural research) or transnational issues (such as river basins and regional infrastructure) might be considered as part of transformational development, depending on the circumstances.

21 As another example, see Bureau for Global Health, "USAID Family Planning Strategic Budgeting Model User Guide," Version 2, September 2005.

Conclusion

Most critiques of U.S. bilateral foreign aid emphasize the problem of policy incoherence—multiple and competing goals and objectives that pull in different directions—leading to real and perceived problems of aid ineffectiveness. This policy addresses these problems by establishing five core strategic goals for bilateral foreign aid. It calls for identifying the resources associated with each goal and managing those resources so as to achieve the best results in terms of each goal.

The policy framework can be implemented by internal measures to align resources in existing accounts with core goals. Those resources are then managed according to the guiding principles for each goal. Although a new set of accounts for foreign aid that correspond to the five core goals would be advantageous, this policy can be implemented under the present account structure.

Annex: Guiding Principles for Effective Assistance

The success of foreign aid in achieving development objectives depends on adherence to a set of principles distilled from over 50 years of experience. Failure to adhere to these principles increases the likelihood of failure. Those listed below are fundamental to the effectiveness of assistance as an instrument of U.S. foreign policy and national security.

Ownership: Development must build on the leadership, participation, and commitment of a country and its people. The role of donor organizations is to support and assist this process as partners working toward a common objective.

Capacity Building: Strong local institutions, a skilled labor force, and appropriate policies are crucial to a country's ability to attract and absorb economic investment, provide public services, facilitate good governance, and manage its own development progress. Thus, capacity building—focused on building local public and private institutions, transferring technical skills, and promoting appropriate policies—is vital to development success.

Sustainability: Development interventions must be appropriate to the capacity of a country or community to sustain them, in terms of its environment, financial resources, economy, institutions, commitment, and human capital. Sustainability must be taken into account during program design and through all phases of implementation.

Accountability: Systems of accountability and transparency, with effective checks and balances, guard against corruption and facilitate economic growth and good governance. Development programs must build and strengthen these systems, institutions, and processes, making them a model for others and ensuring stewardship of public resources.

Assessment: Needs, capacity, cultural norms, and other conditions vary from country to country and community to community. The success of development programs requires that careful research and knowledge of local conditions inform program design. Similarly, best practices imported from experience in other contexts will fail unless they are adapted to local conditions.

Results: The National Security Strategy emphasizes that the United States must "insist upon measurable results to ensure that development assistance is actually making a difference in the lives of the poor." This requires programming resources to achieve clearly defined, measurable, and strategically focused objectives.

Partnership: Development cannot be unilaterally mandated and implemented. Development success requires close collaboration among donors, governments, communities, nongovernmental organizations, the private sector, and universities. Partnerships build ownership and capacity and achieve significant results through joint efforts, based on comparative advantage and common objectives.

Flexibility: Local conditions for development vary widely and can change rapidly—for better or worse. Development agencies must be efficient and flexible: adaptable to local environments and capable of adjusting to changing conditions and seizing opportunities when they arise.

Selectivity: Development resources are limited relative to the world's needs; they are a public asset that must be invested prudently to achieve maximum impact. Assistance allocations among countries should be based on three criteria: need, U.S. foreign policy interests, and the commitment of a country and its leadership to reform. At the country level, resources should be invested where they have maximum impact in achieving priority strategic objectives.

U.S. Agency for International Development

The U.S. Agency for International Development (USAID) is an independent federal agency that receives overall foreign policy guidance from the Secretary of State. For more than 40 years, USAID has been the principal U.S. agency to extend assistance to countries recovering from disaster, trying to escape poverty, and engaging in democratic reforms. USAID supports long-term and equitable economic growth and advances U.S. foreign policy objectives by supporting

- economic growth, agriculture, and trade
- global health
- democracy and conflict prevention
- humanitarian assistance

The Agency's strength is its field offices located in four regions of the world:

- Sub-Saharan Africa
- Asia and the Near East
- Latin America and the Caribbean
- Europe and Eurasia